To my parents, Graham and Margaret, for planting the seeds   A.S-B.
For Steven, Celeste and Daniel Harrison Gomez with love   E.G.

Text copyright © 2007 Anna Scott-Brown
Illustrations copyright © 2007 Elena Gomez
This edition copyright © 2007 Lion Hudson

The moral rights of the author and illustrator
have been asserted

A Lion Children's Book
an imprint of
Lion Hudson plc
Mayfield House, 256 Banbury Road,
Oxford OX2 7DH, England
www.lionhudson.com
ISBN 978 0 7459 6031 9

First edition 2007
1 3 5 7 9 10 8 6 4 2 0

A catalogue record for this book is available
from the British Library

Typeset in 20/28 Throhand Regular
Printed and bound in China

Creation Song

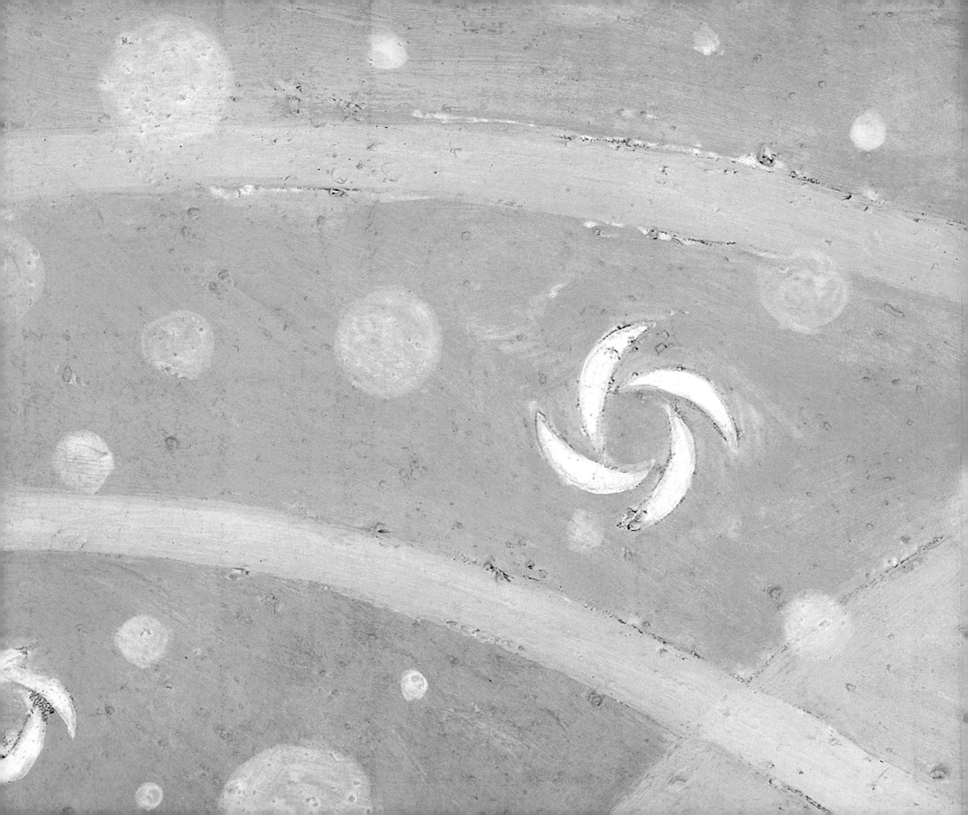

Creation Song

Anna Scott-Brown

Illustrations by Elena Gomez

LION
CHILDREN'S

In the beginning there was God.
And not much else.

In fact, apart from God there was
nothing.

So God was all alone.

But God had a plan...

Out in the silent darkness he began to dream.
He dreamed of friendship and laughter,

of little running streams,
and butterfly wings,
of great mountain slopes
and wind in the trees.

Then, from somewhere deep within,
God started to

S I N G.

And his song spread through the formless deep,
running across the void, carrying the longings of God
as far as they could go.

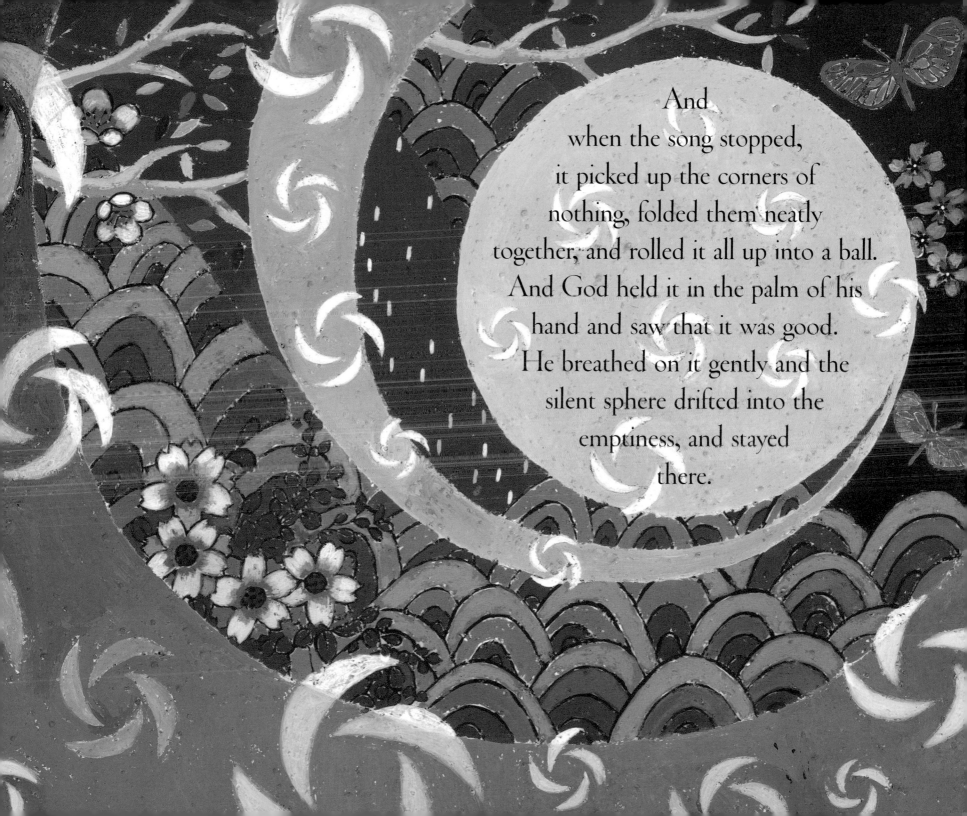

And
when the song stopped,
it picked up the corners of
nothing, folded them neatly
together, and rolled it all up into a ball.
And God held it in the palm of his
hand and saw that it was good.
He breathed on it gently and the
silent sphere drifted into the
emptiness, and stayed
there.

Then with steps as light as the sigh of a moth,
God danced across the surface of nothing.

Everywhere he stepped a tiny prick of light pierced the sleeping shell.
Faster and faster he danced and more and more light broke through.
Something began to stir deep down in the heart of nothing.
It stretched.

A hollow appeared and then a rise.
And instead of nothing there were hills
and there were valleys.

Excitedly all the little points of light
rushed over to see what was happening
and became the

sun.

So God went on
dancing
and created more light –

the stars

and planets.

Then the earth s t r e t c h e d itself
so far
and so wide

that it split apart
and there was land,
and deep chasms.

God cried tears of joy and water poured down
through the holes made by the light, and the
seas and lakes and rivers filled up with water.

Eagerly the sun *hurried* over to see –
and reflected in the water there was the moon.

Gladly the small lights danced as God's tears fell
across the earth in rainbow colours.

From the soil beneath, trees
and plants began to grow.

God and Earth began to laugh, and as their
laughter spread the colour sped before it,
flowers opened, bushes burst into blossom
and on the trees fruit grew.

On and on the laughter flowed
and where it caught a raindrop
birds flew –
of every shape, and size and hue –

and **filled** the earth
with yet more music.

From on high they landed on the
earth, where there were animals of
every kind – great herds of zebras,
gazelles and towering giraffes.

There were flying lizards, running emus,
bleating sheep and calling owls.

And the waters teemed with fish,
leaping and swimming in the
seas and rivers.

God saw that it was good.
So he stepped down and walked on earth.

Then he began to s i n g once more,
deep deep notes from far within.
Every created thing added its own notes to the music,
which rose and filled the air –
and there was man.

Joyfully God went on singing, higher and higher
and the music wrapped itself around man
and brought forth woman.

Then God began to dance and instead of
nothing there were seals and elephants and
chimpanzees, kangaroos and platypus,
big fish and small fish, flat fish and round fish,
peacocks and hoopees, crested birds and humming birds,

and the wind and the trees, flowers and leaves,
the waters and the waves and all good things,
the sun and the moon and the stars.

And at the centre was God with the two beings he had made in his own likeness. They combined within themselves all the music of his soul and all the love of his heart and all the joy of creation.

All creation
danced
with him.

Other titles from Lion Children's Books

The Lion Treasury of Angel Stories   *Mary Joslin & Elena Temporin*

The Jesse Tree   *Geraldine McCaughrean & Bee Willey*

On that Christmas Night   *Mary Joslin & Helen Cann*

Bats are the only mammals that can really fly,
and flight has made them very successful.
There are more than nine hundred species, living in
almost every habitat from subarctic tundra to
tropical forests and deserts. Birds may rule the air
by day, but bats are the monarchs of the night.

This book is about one of the pipistrelle bats.
Pipistrelles are found around the world,
from North America to Africa, Europe,
Asia and Australia.

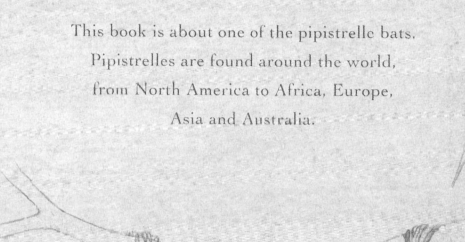

For Henry Venner Woodcock and his big brothers,
Alfie and Thomas
N.D.

For Ailsa
S.F-D.

First published 2001 by Walker Books Ltd
87 Vauxhall Walk, London SE11 5HJ

This edition published 2002

2 4 6 8 10 9 7 5 3 1

Text © 2001 Nicola Davies
Illustrations © 2001 Sarah Fox-Davies

This book was typeset in Cochin and Sanvito

Printed in Hong Kong

British Library Cataloguing in Publication Data:
a catalogue record for this book is available
from the British Library

ISBN 0-7445-9402-2

No ....   Class ....

Author ....

Title ....

BRISTOL CITY COUNCIL LIBRARY SERVICE
PLEASE RETURN BOOK BY LAST DATE STAMPED

Bristol Libraries

Renewals 0845 002 0777
www.bristol-city.gov.uk/libraries

Greater horseshoe bat

(Rhinolophus ferrumequinum)

Greater bulldog bat

(Noctilio leporinus)

White fruit bats

(Ectophylla alba)

Common vampire bat

(Desmodus rotundus)

Spotted bat

(Euderma maculatum)

Hardwickes mouse-tailed bat

(Rhinopoma hardwickei)

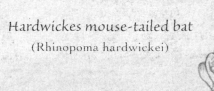

BAT LOVES THE NIGHT

Nicola Davies

illustrated by

Sarah Fox-Davies

WALKER BOOKS
AND SUBSIDIARIES
LONDON · BOSTON · SYDNEY

Bat is waking,
upside down as usual,
hanging by her toenails.

Her beady eyes open.
Her pixie ears twitch.

She shakes her
thistledown fur.

She unfurls her wings,
made of skin so fine the finger bones
inside show through.

This pipistrelle bat
is no bigger than
your thumb.

A bat's wing is its
arm and hand.
Four extra-long fingers
support the skin of the wing.

7

Bats' toes are shaped like hooks,
so it's no effort for a bat to hang
upside down.

Now she unhooks her toes
and drops into black space.
With a sound like a tiny umbrella
opening, she flaps her wings.

Bat is flying.

Out!

Out under the broken tile
into the night-time garden.

Over bushes, under trees,
between fence posts,
through the tangled hedge
she swoops untouched.
Bat is at home in the darkness,
as a fish is in the water.
She doesn't need to see –
she can hear where she is going.

Bats can see. But in the dark, good ears
are more useful than eyes.

Bat shouts as she flies, louder than
a hammer blow, higher than a squeak.
She beams her voice around her like a
torch, and the echoes come singing back.
They carry a sound-picture of all
her voice has touched.
Listening hard, Bat can hear every
detail, the smallest twigs, the
shape of leaves.

Using sound to find your way like this
is called echolocation.
Some bats shout through their mouth,
and some shout through their nose.

14

Gliding and fluttering
back and forth,
she shouts her torch of
sound amongst the trees,
listening for her supper.

All is still...

15

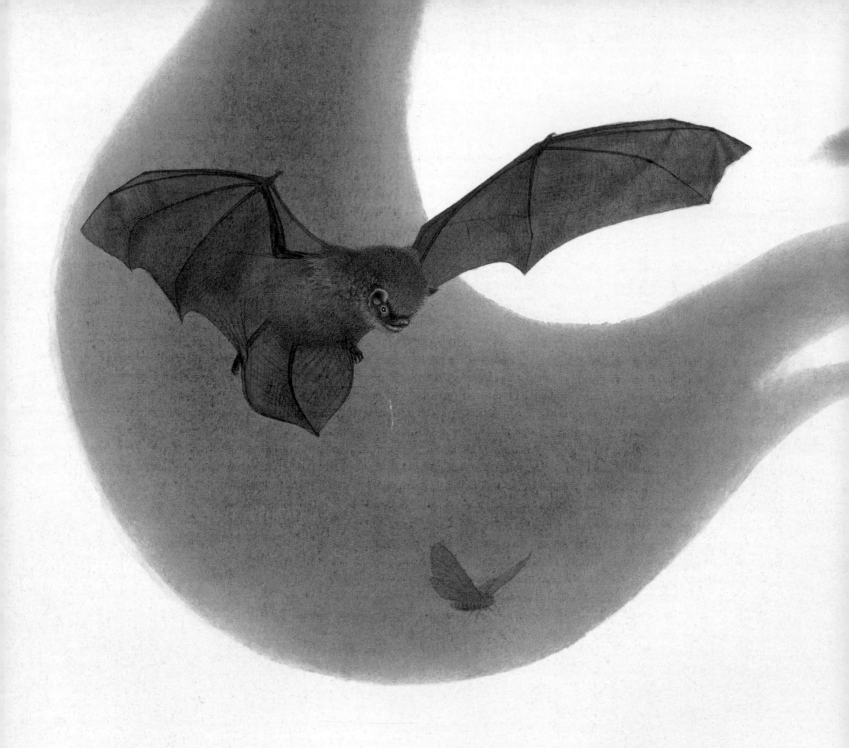

Then a fat moth takes flight below her.

Bat plunges, fast as
blinking, and grabs it in
her open mouth.

But the moth's pearly
scales are moon-dust
slippery. It slithers from
between her teeth.

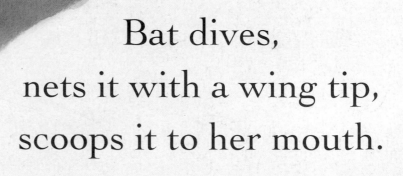

Bat dives,
nets it with a wing tip,
scoops it to her mouth.

This time she bites hard.
Its wings fall away, like the
wrapper from a toffee.
In a moment the moth is eaten.
Bat sneezes.
The dusty scales got up her nose.

Hunting time has run out.
The dark will soon be gone.
In the east the sky is getting light.
It's past Bat's bedtime.

The place where bats sleep in the day is called a roost.
It can be in a building, a cave, or a tree, so long as it's dry and safe.

20

She flies to the roof in the last shadows,
and swoops in under the broken tile.

Inside there are squeakings.
Fifty hungry batlings hang in a huddle,
hooked to a rafter by outsized feet.
Bat lands and pushes in amongst them,
toes first, upside down again.

Baby bats can't fly.
Sometimes mother bats carry their babies when
they go out, but mostly the babies stay behind in the roost
and crowd together to keep warm.

Bat knows her baby's voice, and calls to it.

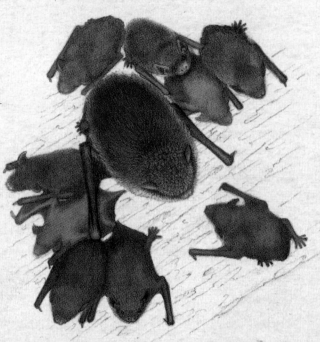

The velvet scrap batling climbs aboard and clings to her fur by its coat-hanger feet.

Wrapped in her
leather wings,
it suckles
Bat's milk.

Baby bats drink mother's milk until
they learn to fly at a few weeks old.
Then they can leave the roost
at night to find their own food.

Outside the birds are singing.
The flowers turn their faces to the sun.
But inside the roof hole,
the darkness stays.
Bat dozes with her batling,
waiting.

Bats are nocturnal. That means they rest by day
and come out at night to search for food.

When the tide of night rises again
Bat will wake, and plunge
into the blackness, shouting.

Bat loves the night.

Index

Look up the pages to find
out about all these batty things.
Don't forget to look at both
kinds of word –
this kind and
this kind.

Mexican freetail bat
(Tadarida brasiliensis)

About the Author

Nicola Davies is a zoologist and has studied all kinds of mammals, from whales in the Indian Ocean and Newfoundland to bats in west Wales. She has written and presented television and radio programmes, and was one of the first presenters on the Bafta Award-winning *The Really Wild Show*. Nowadays she writes books for adults and children. Among her books for children are three other Walker titles: *Big Blue Whale*, *One Tiny Turtle* and *Wild About Dolphins*.

About the Illustrator

Sarah Fox-Davies has illustrated many picture books for children, including *Walk with a Wolf* by Janni Howker, which was shortlisted for the the Kurt Maschler Award and Highly Commended for the Times Educational Supplement Junior Information Book of the Year Award; and *Little Beaver and the Echo* by Amy MacDonald, which was shortlisted for the Children's Book Award.

NOTES FOR TEACHERS

The READ AND WONDER series is an innovative and versatile resource for reading, thinking and discovery. Each book invites children to become excited about a topic, see how varied information books can be, and want to find out more.

👉 **Reading aloud** The story form makes these books ideal for reading aloud – in their own right or as part of a cross-curricular topic, to a child or to a whole class. After you've introduced children to the books in this way, they can revisit and enjoy them again and again.

👉 **Shared reading** Big Book editions are available for several titles, so children can read along, discuss the topic, and comment on the different ways information is presented – to wonder together.

👉 **Group and guided reading** Children need to experience a range of reading materials. Information books like these help develop the skills of reading to learn, as part of learning to read. With the support of a reading group, children can become confident, flexible readers.

👉 **Paired reading** It's fun to take turns to read the information in the main text or captions. With a partner, children can explore the pages to satisfy their curiosity and build their understanding.

👉 **Individual reading** These books can be read for interest and pleasure by children at home and in school.

👉 **Research** Once children have been introduced to these books through reading aloud, they can use them for independent or group research, as part of a curricular topic.

👉 **Children's own writing** You can offer these books as strong models for children's own information writing. They can record their observations and findings about a topic, make field notes and sketches, and add extra snippets of information for the reader.

Above all, Read and Wonders are to be enjoyed, and encourage children to develop a lasting curiosity about the world they live in.

Sue Ellis, Centre for Language in Primary Education